Floating and Sinking

Sue Barraclough

Raintree

Chicago, Illinois

Customer Service   888–454–2279

Visit our website at www.heinemannlibrary.com

Photo research by Ruth Blair, Erica Newbery, and Kay Altwegg
Designed by Jo Hinton-Malivoire and bigtop design ltd
Printed and bound in China by South China Printing Company
10 09 08 07 06
10 9 8 7 6 5 4 3 2 1

Library of Congress Cataloging-in-Publication Data
Barraclough, Sue.
  Floating and sinking / Sue Barraclough.
    p. cm. -- (How do things move?)
  Includes bibliographical references and index.
  ISBN 1-4109-2259-6 (library binding-hardcover) -- ISBN 1-4109-2264-2 (pbk.)
  1. Floating bodies--Juvenile literature. I. Title.
  QC147.5.B37 2006
  532'.25--dc22

                              2005029585

Acknowledgments
The author and publisher are grateful to the following for permission to reproduce copyright
material: Alamy pp. **6, 22 bottom** (Brand X Pictures), **11** (Sarkis Images), **12** (RubberBall),
18, 23 top left (Dave Porter), **19, 23 top right** (Stephen Frink Collection), **20, 22 top left**
(Danita Delimont); Corbis pp. **9** (Peter Barrett), **10, 22 top right** (Ariel Skelley), **14** (Craig
Lovell), **16, 17** (Rolf Bruderer); Getty Images (Photodisc) pp. **7, 13, 21, 23 bottom**; Nature
Picture Library p. **15** (Doc White); Photolibrary p. **8** (Index Stock Imagery); Punchstock p. **4,
5** (RF).

Cover photograph reproduced with permission of Corbis (Stuart Westmorland).

Some words are shown in bold, **like this**. You can find out
what they mean by looking in the glossary.

Contents

Floating

If something stays on top of water, it floats.

4

These children are floating in a swimming pool.

Sinking

If something goes under water, it sinks.

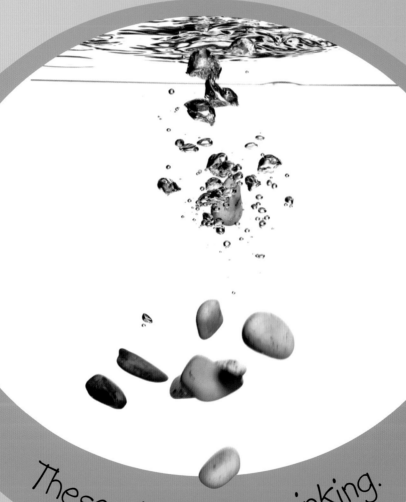

These stones are sinking.

This boat has a hole. It is sinking, too.

Helping You Float

There are a lot of things to help you float on water.

Floating Fun

There are a lot of ways to have fun floating on water.

Floating in a boat can be fun.
The air in this **raft** helps it float.

Sinking Fun

Swimming underwater can be fun, too.

This **diver** has special **gear** so she can stay underwater longer.

Animals in Water

This otter can float on water.

It can
dive down
underwater, too.

15

Skipping Stones

Skipping stones is fun!

Plop!

Flat stones can bounce on water. Then they sink down under the water.

Light and Heavy

This beach ball is filled with air. It is light. It floats on water.

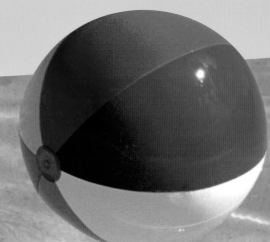

This **anchor** is heavy.
It sinks under water.

19

What Do You Think?

This is a boat.

Do you think it will float or sink?

100358

This is a bicycle.

Do you think it will float or sink?

Floating or Sinking?

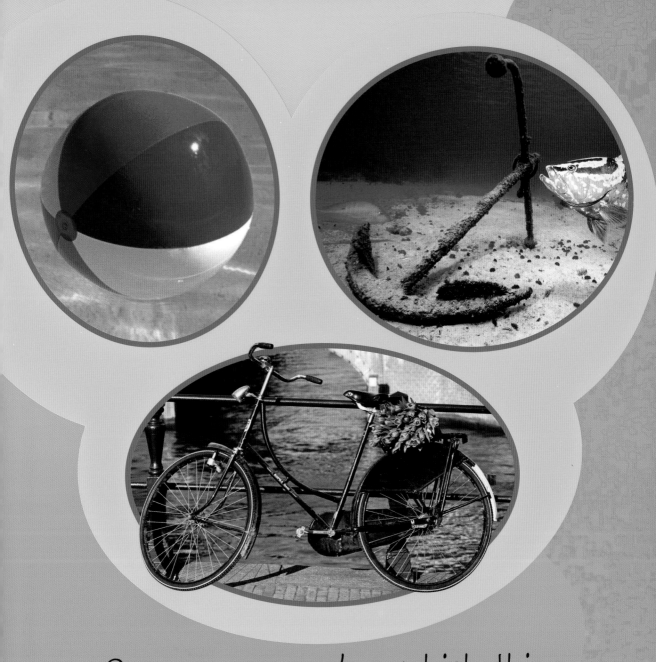

Can you remember which things
float and which things sink?

Glossary

anchor *keeps a boat still*

gear *objects used to do a job*

diver *person who dives*

raft *flat object that floats*

Index

Notes for Adults

The *How Do Things Move?* series provides young children with a first opportunity to learn about motion. Each book encourages children to notice and ask questions about the types of movement they see around them.

These books will also help children extend their vocabulary, as they will hear some new words. Since words are used in context in the book this should enable young children to gradually incorporate them into their own vocabulary.

Follow-up activities
- Ask your child to look around the house and identify three things that will float and three things that will sink. Then find out whether he or she is right by testing each item in a bowl of water together.
- Demonstrate how filling something with air can make it float by placing a blown-up balloon in a bowl of water alongside a balloon that has not been blown up. Ask your child to guess what is making the difference.